EMILY'S JOURNEY 01 - MY MEMORY

Feng-Yi

BALBOA.
PRESS
A DIVISION OF HAY HOUSE

Balboa Press books may be ordered through booksellers or by contacting:

Balboa Press
A Division of Hay House
1663 Liberty Drive
Bloomington, IN 47403
www.balboapress.com.au
1-(877) 407-4847

ISBN: 978-1-4525-0479-7 (sc)
ISBN: 978-1-4525-0480-3 (e)

Printed in the United States of America

Balboa Press rev. date: 05/08/2012

CONTENTS

SUFFERER AND CONQUEROR

It is a cloudy day. Emily arrives at class early, as usual. That day's lesson is on English pronunciation. This class is quite popular; unfortunately, no more than twenty students can take it at a time.

She likes to be alone, so she sits in a corner as another classmate arrives. She keeps her head down to avoid talking to the classmate. She is quite shy. She finds it difficult even just to say hi.

Emily enjoys school, and she believes that everyone in the class is the teacher's most important asset. She also likes teachers who encourage a healthy learning environment that the students enjoy being in.

As a student, Emily also thinks that she is an important part of the class, so she makes every reasonable effort to ensure that she respects her classmates and listens when they speak; that she respects their rights as individuals; and that she treats them in a fair and equal way at all times. In return, she expects that her classmates will respect her and listen to her; that they will respect her rights as an individual; and that they will treat her in a fair and equal way at all times.

Despite her efforts to treat her classmates with respect, one of her classmates bullies her that day. The classmate makes her feel like a disabled girl who she should be in a special centre because she requires special care. The classmate says hurtful things like, "You can't be dress by yourself; you need someone to feed you like a dog." The classmate pushes Emily down.

Emily looks around her and sees nothing real. She is tired of everything. She is physically exhausted and just wants to escape that classmate. Her initial reaction is to forgive her classmate and then maybe get to a point where she can love her classmate again, even when her classmate is hurting her, but it is not that easy.

She understands that most people have opinions about individuals or groups of people who are different from them. This is quite natural and a part of human nature.

These opinions are formed early in our lives. Starting from a young age, we start to decide what's *normal* and what's *different*. Our parents also contribute to our opinions, though when we become adults we might make different decisions about *normal* and *different*.

Emily has known she is quite different from others since she was a little girl, but she doesn't deserve this sort of prejudice. She enjoys the class, but her timid personality can't stand up against the sort of treatment her classmate has inflicted on her. She also doesn't want to give teachers and classmates any trouble, so what should she do?

Perhaps you have been a victim in a situation like Emily's. If so, you know that it can be hurtful and destructive to feel this way.

Anyway, she pretends that she has left. She pretends she is not in that classroom. She pretends none of the bad things have happened. She pretends it is okay, but it never lasts. It just seems like a waste of time, because pretending does not make her happy and she gets so tired of smiling at everyone.

As Emily gets home, she feels stuck and spends most of her time crying and punching walls. Sometimes she goes as far as making her knuckles bleed. She is hurt. She is angry. She is lost, and she is alone.

Dear reader, as you read up to here, you might think that there are still people in this world who don't realise or worst still don't care that bullying still exists. In a group, if there is someone who is suffering, there must also be someone who takes the part of comforter. You must be a comforter as you read through Emily's suffering.

Thank you, reader.

PRAY

Emily knows that she could change her life for the better if she worked really hard at it. But now it's time for her excuses for not going back to class since her classmate knocked her down. She decides to attend the Individual Learning Centre (ILC) instead of attending the English class.

The Individual Learning Centre is located within the library. Students can come to the ILC at any time. It provides assistance to meet each student's needs, such as computer programs, workshops, reading, and writing letters, essays, and reports.

She is trying so hard to make her life better from today on, but it looks like the weather is going to frustrate her. She decides to get her personal errands done early in the morning, as she will not be able endure the very high temperatures after 11.00 a.m.

Emily is very good at organizing things. She writes on notes the chores that she needs to do so that she won't forget any of them. That way she can get things done more efficiently.

She finished her personal errands and arrives on time for the afternoon ILC class.

She enjoys the afternoon class at first, but a text message from someone she does not know well but who cares about her makes her want to cry. The message reads: I Will Pray For You.

She wishes she could cry. She wishes she could pray to a god. She wants to believe that when she wakes up tomorrow, she won't have to see how fake her reactions are because she received that message. It was sent by one of her classmates in English pronunciation class. They hardly to talk, even just to say hi.

Unfortunately, she hides these feeling.

Emily's true reaction is completely the opposite of what people see when she arrives at school. They say to her, "Look at you, smiling and a happy face. You seem happy all the time." This makes her feel so much worse, because she is in a very different mood when she is alone. There isn't a single person in the world she can talk to. She has especially felt recently that something is missing in her life, as if the world has swooped her up and she stopped being creative. She feels so alone and so hopeless all the time. She tries her best to hide it, but as time goes on, the sensation simply get worse and worse. She did have a group of friends when she was a child, and in school she had good, professional teachers, but now she has no one she can really talk to. She has found it too difficult to make friends as she's grown older. It is a stupid thing to do, but she sometimes entertains the thought of killing herself because she has no one talk to.

One of the suicide methods she has thought about is drowning. She knows drowning is not painful, because she almost drowned once. When she was five, her brother pushed her into the swimming pool. To drown, a person only has to submerge herself in water to prevent breathing and deprive the brain of oxygen. Of course, due to the body's natural tendency to come up for air, a person trying to drown often has to use a heavy object to overcome this reflex. Or they need to be someone like Emily, who really can't swim.

She has life insurance, so she has also thinks a car crash could be a good way to end her life.

The percentage of car accidents that are actually suicides is unknown. The research shows that even when suicide is suspected, if there is no suicide note, the fatal crash will be classified an accident.

So Emily wonders if drowning or a car accident would be good for her.

She has been feeling this way for years and she needs it to stop. She needs a friend to let her release the painful things she feels inside and all the stress they cause, or she believes she really can't last much longer.

Because she acts the way that people like, others can't guess how she feels. No one really understands her points of view about things, her thoughts about life in general. But why does she have so much stress?

Emily is a lonely girl, indeed. And because she has always been shy, she has difficulty talking about her feelings, even with someone whom she thinks would care or who might try to help her. That is why she thinks writing is good for her. Writing lets her try to get back to what she loves, to find happiness in everyday things, and it is something she is capable of doing. Although she isn't really sure where she should start in the story of her life, she knows that if she doesn't write it down, it will be locked inside her forever, eating away at her soul.

Remark: Emily is a little less than a quarter of a century in years. That sounds young, but considers this: she has no friends, she is a lonely girl, and she is trying to change her life for the better.

BROKEN WINGS (AUTISTIC)

Emily moves to the Individual Learner Centre in the campus library, and it is full of students from different cultural backgrounds. She thinks that the students in the ILC do not judge her. They do not try to fight her, so she loves to stay there.

Sometimes, though, as she sits for the longest time in the ILC, she feels so ugly in her skin that she can't bear it. The only friend she has now is her journal. So one day she takes her journal out, but she doesn't write a new entry. She reviews previous ones.

One of the journal entries that attracts her begins as follows:

1—Why do I get amnesia after I release the pressure?

2—Why do I get headaches after I release the pressure?

3—Why do I hear my pulse when I kneel down and the
    ligature tightens?

That entry reminds Emily that she was nearly autistic
at that time, and at other times. Those times were so
depressing, and she talked even less than before.

It made her cry when she talked about these depressing
and sad things. She didn't want to see a counsellor or a
doctor because she didn't believe talking would solve her
problems. It would just make her think about them. But
she supposed someone like that could help her find a way
to cope with her feelings better.

And she has had it rough since her dad passed away four
years ago from lung cancer. People told her she shouldn't
complain, because the only thing preventing her from
having her life the way she wanted it to be was *her*. But she
had so many obstacles to overcome. She simply wanted
not to have to worry and to live happily.

She was just so tired, you know? Not physically exhausted,
but tired of life. All the pleasure in her life had run out of
her. Her dad was her shining light; he was her lifeline. She
would have killed herself one night if she hadn't thought
of him. She was going to hang herself, but she got scared
of the pain. She was so serious a long time ago. She was
going to make a will and hide it until that day, when she'd
set it out for someone to see. She wrote a lot about her
feelings and showed them to the friends she'd had then, as
well as teachers, but then she got scared that they would
make her commit herself to a hospital.

Emily's Journey 01 – My Memory

It has been a drastic and emotional time for Emily. Her social life is almost dead. She doesn't know how she can improve her life, and fears she will be like this forever. Always scraping by and watching others succeed in life, while she never catches a break.

Emily has a sudden thought and writes it down in her journal as quick as she can, so that she won't forget.

> Although I have a pair of broken wings, I am going to try to make everyone believe that everything is fine with me now. It doesn't matter that things are getting worse and worse. I am going to try to make everyone believe that I'll be all right. And it doesn't matter how much I want to end my life, I keep my journal on and on. If no one can think of what to tell me or what advice to give me through reading my journal, then hearing me out is the best thing they can do for me.

It sounds as if Emily is trying to be a fairy that doesn't have wings, and is trying to bring intimate harmony to every moment.

It is impossible for me as a reader to go to the place where Emily sings. I hope she will get better in all things.

UNBALANCE THE SYSTEM ESCAPE

The weather has been frustrating recently, just like now. The sky is clear, but then the clouds cover it in five minutes. The electricity is extinguished in a second, and then it starts to rain. Although the rain hits Emily so hard, it catches her heart so simply. She wonders if it can tear her world apart.

Emily wanders around the campus, angry at the weather. Although the rain pitches at her so hard, she tries to sing to it and to fly into the darkness with her broken wings, because no one likes a sad girl. Think about the quiet girl you knew in school. Was she sad because she had no friends? Emily believes melancholic young women make others uncomfortable, because being sad, genuinely unhappy, is a denial of a profound message of always being upbeat that is sent to all girls.

It is not easy to be around unhappy people.

She has not been the happiest child since primary school. She was not looking for sympathy, she was not looking for attention, but attention was what she got. Peers and teachers alike openly expressed their annoyance with Emily's introversion.

She didn't get it. Why was her personality and behaviour so offensive? What rule was she breaking?

Meanwhile, the popular girls around her giggled, shrieked, and guffawed about nothing in particular. The stupidest joke made by a friend or a boy would send them into gales of cruel laughter.

She understands why teenage girls laugh at everything and anything, why they never stop smiling and always keep the conversation light.

There is absolutely nothing wrong with being unhappy, emotive, and quiet.

Nowadays, society seems to be losing touch with the internal voice, the emotional intuition that tells us how we truly feel. So while others tell you to cheer up, your internal voice says, Cheer up . . . if you want to. Be who you are. Well, Emily would like to be who she is from now on, although she has always lived in her own world. It is small, but it has all she really needs. It is her favourite place to visit. In her favourite place, she creates lots imaginative stories and fantasies. Please don't think that she could be alone forever in her own world that her face is on a frieze that never ends, and that she would travel in her mind towards death. She is just fine, and she appreciates that although others outside her world have always cared about her, they cannot be the sun to end her night. Still, she is sure that they will watch her until its light.

"Oh, light," Emily whispers.

Angel must have known that Emily needs light, so while Emily is dancing in the rain, the power comes back on. It is fortunate for Emily, for now can go into the ILC to do her work. She writes down in her journal all of her thoughts and feelings about this unbalance in the system. In the last sentence, she writes, "I am what I am, and I will show them that *I am* and I exist in their perfect system just to unbalance their stupid equation." Then she closes her journal and goes for a walk.

Please don't think that Emily wants to escape out of this "real world" into another world. She just wants to be refreshed and enjoy life. Well, she has always enjoyed simple things in life, like now. A walk in a park, eating good takeaway food, reading a book, watching a movie she likes. She doesn't want to be rich. She just wants to have an ordinary job that pays enough money for her food and bills, or find a husband to create a lovely family with. All of her classmates, neighbours and others she knew seemed ahead of their time, trying to accelerate their evolution, both physically and mentally. That is, being an adult before becoming an adult, like losing their innocence at very young ages. Unfortunately for them, Emily represents this obstacle to being grown up, for when she was a teenager; she never tried to act like a serious adult.

HEARTY SMILE

Although it is a dull day, Emily still goes to the ILC. It sounds kind of numbing, the kind of numbing that puts you in a perpetual fog and makes you want to sleep all day, but she still goes to the ILC.

Emily sits in a corner of the ILC area, feeling sad as usual but with a smiling face. She has been depressed recently. As classmates keep arriving, she pretends she is fine and smiles at them, and even has a little chat, but then there are moments of weakness when she is left alone.

Is it embarrassing for others to learn how to acknowledge your personality or to tell you indirectly that you are the problem? The answer is obvious to Emily.

Emily, unfortunately, has a mother and a naughty brother who blame her for everything. They scream at her, push her, and so on. For the longest time she thought she was the problem. So when thoughts of suicide arrive, she is not surprised anymore.

Our society really needs to be more accepting and compassionate of people like Emily.

Emily has positive thoughts all the time and would like to live for the betterment of herself and for those around her. She doesn't understand why most people, instead of asking her why she is so quiet, why she talks so softly and act so strangely, they go out of their way—every single adult—to chide her because she isn't super smart. They blame her for being "so difficult" or "so different." They practically abandoned her when she really needed help the most, or embarrassed her instead of trying to understand her, and that made her think most people her age weren't so nice either.

Poor Emily. All of her classmates think she is stupid, that she is useless. She loves God, but she doesn't have the assurance that he is there. What if her God is not real? What if God is not there? She feels terrible even thinking these things. What if all of mankind is fighting to go to somewhere wonderful after death, but there's nowhere, nothing, zero? She can't live like this. Her mum saying she is a disappointment all the time, her brother saying she has got no brain and that everything would be better if she died. She would like someone to save her! Tell her there's something to live for! She wants to live for God, but how? She can't act! She can't sing! She can't even communicate with him! She is so down all the time. *All the time!*

Whenever Emily's mind is assaulted by these thoughts, she tries to fight against it, even though she can't define what "it" really is. She puts up a front, always smiling like a Little Mary Sunshine, even though her heart is breaking and her life is in the toilet, because she thinks that's what good girls do. She worries that one day she will come home exhausted just from smiling!

Anyway, Emily is a very sweet girl. Although she has been feeling okay most of the time, she suffers moments of weakness when she is alone. When thoughts of sadness arrive in her mind, she is not surprised that she loses her innocent smile that she feels she is only on the verge of life.

Although she thinks she can't handle it anymore, she returns to the ILC and sits in a corner. She writes in her journal, reads books, and listens to others. She gives advice sometimes when someone talks to her about her problems, and she believes herself when she says, "Everything's going to be okay," but she doesn't believe it when someone tells her the same thing.

Although I'm so lonely and there will always be obstacles to overcome, I can shape and mould the life that I want, and I can learn a lot from obstacles. And yet I thoroughly believe in God. But I don't believe that God wants me to spend my life searching for it. Although the pain will never go away and the wound will never heal, God is in me and angels are all around me, just like the movie says."

That is the last line in Emily's journal that day.

EMILY 06
PRESSURE

The pressures that surround Emily every day are now keeping her from getting out of bed in the morning. For some reason it's impossible to get a job where she lives. She hasn't gone to class in weeks and she feels she is too far behind to catch up. Everything is crumbling around her and she feels hopeless. She can't summon the strength to get up in the morning and walk twenty minutes down the street to sit in class. She has been completely antisocial lately.

These feelings aren't going to go away. No one in this world would hire a girl, even though she's desperate for a job, because of her slow, struggling way of speaking and her soft, slow movements. No one is going to make her mother love her, or make her brother nice and want to have a relationship with her. She has nothing left to care about; there is nothing left for her here. She can feel herself getting weaker and weaker and caring less and less about everything in her life. She is not heartless; she is just so lost and so depressed. She doesn't think she will ever find her way.

She can't remember when she became depressed. Was it before or after she started dropping her classes? If before, when was the first time she can remember feeling depressed? Was it from something internal? Whatever the reason, this is a conflict she must resolve within herself.

She remembers that when she was young, everyone said, "Life isn't fair. Get used to it." Well, they were right. As she looks back she sees good times and bad times, but the good times only account for about 5 percent of life. The rest is either shit or even worse, so most of Emily's life passes like a dream, and it reveals only what is in her mind. She hopes she can unravel seams and release something one day.

Life overwhelming her much of the times. She tries to think that she is not alone going through these emotions, but she wakes up on her bed with pain. Although she knows she is not supposed to be in the Individual Learning Centre, she walks the twenty minutes to get there and sits quietly in a corner. Actually, she doesn't fit in anywhere. She doesn't fit with her mum. She doesn't fit with her brother. She doesn't fit with her neighbour. She doesn't fit with her classmates. She hopes this isn't getting worse and worse.

"Would you like to see a counsellor about your career?" a teacher in the ILC asks Emily suddenly.

Emily just smiles and shakes her head.

She doesn't want to see any counsellor about anything, because most counsellors just make patients talk to them and then go talk to another one. It sounds stupid, doesn't it? To tell the same thing, the same story, from the start many times to different counsellors, and the patient doesn't get better. So Emily does not want to see any counsellors and tell her story over and over again. Actually, she doesn't feel good enough to talk about anything. She is sitting in the campus library and just reading, writing in her journal, and typing up stories.

Does it seem Emily's life is finally on track? She does not know. At least she has found things she likes to do and she has found things that she likes about herself. It sounds as if she has many good qualities and different things that she would like to do, but that doesn't mean she likes all of them.

Does it seem that Emily has explored her mind a bit? Yes, she has, and she writes all her explorations down in her journal.

At last she writes: "I guess I should tell you all that my dream job is to become a writer, although I don't know how many words I need beyond the sea. Whether in love, laughter, different kinds of thoughts, it is unravelling my seam with luck."

LIFE

On this very hot day, Emily thought, *Accept it when life is a challenge. Solve it when life is a challenge. Play it when life is a game. Complete it when life is a journey. But remember life is what you make it.*

It sounds easy, but it actually is not. Life is never easy for a girl like Emily, soft and weak, so she accepts it when life is a challenge. Unfortunately, she can't solve it, but she absolutely believes that "Life is what I make it."

All my life is making decisions, she thought. Every day, with every step she chooses, the direction changes.

Sometimes it's hard. Life is much harder now that she is an adult. One step can change a range of events.

For example, she has to decide now—go to the library and write out lots of stories, so she can make money from writing; or listen to others talking and laughing; or just push the button on the computer and watch her future online. She guesses that is the meaning of life.

All her decisions can bring her success in life or not, and she shouldn't blame others, because she is an adult now. Sometimes knowing that feels like a stone on her head, but probably it's the funniest part of life—decisions.

Before each step, Emily should think twice. Like in some Indian tribes in old America, when they made decisions, they wondered about the consequences to *seven* generations! That's what she calls managing life!

She thinks that sometimes, when she can't find her way by using her brain, she needs to follow her heart.

"Cool!" she whispers. It is really cool in the library, especially on this very hot day.

Emily sits in her quiet corner. She opens her journal and starts to write:

> What should I do when my mum is crazy? Hysterical? What should I do when I really hate my mum? She used to snoop through my room and then disappear, no matter how hard I tried to keep her away. Although we are trying to stay distant from each other now, I feel she is still watching me sometimes. I often have to search for her until I feel much safer, so that she is not whispering in my ear when

I'm in the class, when I'm walking, or when I'm sleeping. Sometimes, I wonder if I could change my name to Terra because it means earth and that is my element. I feel Terra inside me often. I used to write in a journal to let out her emotions, so she could tell me she loves me and to tell me what is right and wrong. Could I forget about my pretend personality of Terra and become her someday? Perhaps I could be reincarnated, or go into a never ending dream about my plans when that day has come. I think I've really gotten into what I am writing, and now I am thinking I will stand in the blue sky and burning sun and dream of things only I am capable of. Then maybe one day soon I won't have to worry as much about my difficulties: social problems, facing my mum, and facing my past. Maybe after that, then I can finally rest in peace. If I don't go publicly insane again.

At the end, Emily writes, "Good luck to me. I wish I had thought about my choices, I mean really thought at a deep level before acting in many situations, and good luck to everybody, I hope what I decide turns out to be what I needed. I deserve a good life. Sometimes there isn't enough time to ponder. Hopefully life sends me an extra helping of whatever I need."

Emily closes her journal. She goes to a stationary shop. She wants to buy a new journal, because her current journal has only twenty-five more pages left. Her journey is not finished yet, and she would like to have the new journal ready for when she gets to the last page of the current journal.

She is tired when she gets home. She has no energy. She lies down on her sweet bed and whispers good night to herself. Soon she will write the next page in her journal.

EMILY 08

LOST INNOCENT
(HE RUINED HER LIFE)

Emily can't remember when she started to see the psychologist and talk about her problems. The first psychologist sent her to see a second psychologist. The second psychologist made her talk to him and then to a third one. The third one sent her to a fourth psychologist . . . She stopped telling her whole story after seeing eight psychologists. To tell the story from the start eight times didn't get her far. She got really tired of telling the story over and over again, but she realized that the story wasn't in her journal.

Would I like to have that story in my journal? she asks herself. The answer is definitely *yes*.

It sounds strange that she wants to put all that sadness and cruelty in her journal.

She sits alone in the ILC. She opens her journal and picks from her pen case a lovely pen that she often uses. But the question that keeps running through her head is: Where do I start?

It should start with:

"There are lots of girls who are physically abused by their family members in this society."

It is so sad that Emily was one of those terrible statistics, a girl who was physically, verbally, emotionally, and sexually abused by her family members.

All of Emily's life has given her surprises. She comes from a middle-class family. She couldn't get everything she wanted, but she was happy—until the financial situation at home changed drastically.

She remembers something happened one gloomy day. She had lain down to take a short nap that afternoon. She didn't understand what bothered her as lay awake in bed. But then she heard him approach, heard him open the door.

He walked in, careful not to make the door screech. He stood over her shaking form, and he knew she was awake. She wondered what her mum and her dad would think if they found out. If she woke up at night, she wondered where he was at the moment. She wondered if her mum and her dad knew their son did that to her.

That was one of the dirtiest and cruellest things that had happened to her.

One afternoon, she thought about running away. She packed a bag and sneaked out the front door. She ran to the park with the hard, cold raining hitting her bare arms. At the time she was twelve years old. She had no friends. No phone. No money. Two hours later, she decided to go home to face the horrible thing, since she was scared of living on the street. She thought about suicide. She tried to hang herself once, but it didn't work. She was too scared to cut her wrists. She was scared of failing at suicide, so she lived in a silent, secret hell.

She knows she gets emotional these days since she dropped the English course. If she stays home alone, she likes to sit in the corner of the kitchen, or in the bathroom, or in the living room. She does nothing, just rocks back and forth and smiles.

She is mature for her age. In fact, she is more mature than she is supposed to be. Sometimes that's good. For example, when people argue with each other, she tells them good things about the other. She thinks that we shouldn't hurt others, but help them.

Other times, though, it's bad being mature. Because she doesn't act like other girls her age, she sees through their excuses and lies. She sees them being not real, sees them trying to impress everybody by being like everyone else. She doesn't have many friends because of that. She doesn't want to be friends with someone who is always acting and fake. So it's a struggle every day for her to choose how to react to certain situations. By the way, she didn't read any of this after she wrote it, so if it's horrible, she is sorry. She just wants to know if she will ever be happy.

Will the grass ever be green enough for me? she asks herself as she closes the journal.

SUICIDE IS SELFISH AND EMPTY

What entry should I write in my journal today? Emily asks herself as she sits in her quiet corner of the library and lets the time go by.

It seems that her mind is empty and the blood will not congeal.

Since Emily became a victim of abuse by a member of her family, her world changed forever. Perhaps the library is her world now. She wants to have love from others, but she never expects to be loved by her abuser. Nor does she expect her abuser to turn their relationship into something merciful, so she tries to disappear and find her own way to carry on, but every way she turns there are no answers. Every time she gets near to a resolution, the door slams shut one way or another.

"How are you?" A teacher's voice wakes up her mind. "What would you like to do today?" the teacher asks.

"Oh! I'm just going to do some writing and reading," Emily answers softly.

As the teacher walks away, Emily takes out her journal. She opens it and starts to write.

> All my life is black. I spend most of my time on my own now. At the moment, life is going very wrong. I don't attend any classes anymore, as I am still recovering from my past. I cut myself sometimes, usually more than once a day, and even more than once each time. My mum and my brother don't want me to be happy. I have no friends, and at school they only ever talk to me out of pity. I've hated my life ever since my brother did so many terrible things to me. I am not smart like I used to be, I used to get very good marks, but not now that I am at the college level. Stupid and embarrassing memories are making my life hell. Most people aren't bothered by embarrassing things they said when they were young, but I am. It makes everything even more horrible. I feel total apathy most of the time, and when it isn't apathy, it's relentless sadness. But I have finally found the solution: if there is no life, there is no horrible life. That's why I

started this journal, because I have found the solution, and the solution is suicide.

Suicide. Such a beautiful word to the ears of the depressed, the hopeless, the desperate. You might say someone like me has the perfect life. I have enough food, enough money to buy nice clothes, I can go to school. Well, I should be happy because I have all that. I do not live in some country in Africa with no food, dirty water, no school, and no family at all. The truth, though, is that I am not happy. Do I feel guilty about this? Well, that's actually quite an interesting question. I guess I should, but I don't. I realize there are people with much worse lives than I who want to keep on living. But those people are all right in the head. No psychotic past, no apathy or relentless sadness all the time. They want to continue living because they're not messed up in the head. Sure, their physical lives are horrible, but I'm pretty sure their lives aren't as much of a hell as the lives of the people who are messed up in the head. Anyway, I find it difficult to get motivated with anything apart from my Dad. And I live my life for my dad now. When I write in this journal, I am writing for him. I do things for him, even when I am shut away in the corner of a quiet place, barely speaking to anyone all day. I am still a weak girl. My phone never rings, the only e-mails I get are spam, and I have had enough. I hate the area I live in, but I can't move away as I am scared of losing the memory of my dear daddy. The only thing keeping me going is that my daddy's things adore me as I do him.

A few months ago, I started selling my stuff off bit by bit. It was almost like in preparation of killing myself. I have thought about who would be at my funeral. A good neighbour, a couple of nice classmates, some teachers. I have really wished to be dead every single day since I lost my innocence. You may think that I should try to do something about my life, that I should try to make it better. Well, I have tried. I write things down in my journal and I let ILC teachers read them, but that doesn't work. All the classmates and teachers who helped me in the past don't seem to want to keep in touch, since their lives are all going well, last time I heard. I am still on medications, which end up hurting me in the short run. I go to school like now and try to feel better about myself, but I just end up making a fool of myself because I share too many personal things with too many teachers. I just don't think that life is for me. I don't know why I am writing this so honestly in my journal, but as I do, it shows me how crappy things are and it almost makes the decision in my head a lot clearer.

Although I have thought about suicide many times, the interesting thing is that I have never thought about using hard drugs to escape life.

Just before my decision was made, I felt very confused all the time, because I didn't know how to sort out my affection for my abuser with the sick and disgusting things he did to me. Luckily, I had a good daddy and a good grandmother then. They took good care of me when those things happened to me. And luckily, I have a good listener now, my dear journal.

I know I have forgiven them, but I have never have really forgotten about it. All I want is to experience my first love like everyone else. All I ever wanted was to be accepted for who I am and what I am. Everything I ever believed in fell apart after the abuse, and after so many years, the pain is the same. After forgiveness, I should forget, right? But it is very hard for me to move on. This is the bitterness inside me that I have been dealing with for the past years. Maybe this is why I am such a psycho sometimes.

Honestly, I don't know how to end this. I feel so jealous whenever I see girls my age having a great and happy family. I feel so alone. I am a little less than a quarter of a century in years, but I have no friends. I have always been totally alone. I am totally isolated. I also have immense self-hatred. Every morning that I wake up, I am angry. I am so angry that I am given another day while someone else who might have so much more to live for has died of cancer.

The fact of the matter is, I really hate my life. I feel like I am slowly losing my mind. I have no motivation for life.

Although I have been suicidal for a long time now, one of the reasons I just can't bring myself to do it is that it's such a selfish act. No matter how lonely I may feel, or how much I hate myself, my suicide would have an extremely negative effect on my family. My mother and brother especially would have to deal with the embarrassment along with the guilt. That isn't fair to me, because I cause myself enough embarrassment. So, I thought it was time for my excuses now.

It might sound funny, because I have my suicide supplies with me, but I haven't used them yet.

Suicide indeed is selfish. Asking someone else to bear his or her pain for my sake is also selfish. It's all a matter of who gets that way—you, or those people who claim to care for you, be they true or otherwise. At least I have tried to keep my journal going, just like now, and not do drugs. Writing gets me through such things. I just hope that I have the strength to hold on, hope that I will find the right position, the right place where I can get on with my life and put all the past behind me.

As soon as Emily put the full stop mark after the last sentence, it's time for her to go home.

PLAYAWAY

Well, these unfair and ruined things are all in the past.

Emily is living alone and somewhat happier now.

She has got good company: Playaway.

Playaway is an audio book and player all in one. It comes preloaded with an unabridged book and is ready to play whenever you are.

Emily's dad used to buy her audio cassettes together with a storybook. They accompanied her throughout her childhood. Now, she still relies on them since she has no friends.

It is hard to buy audio cassettes nowadays, which is so sad. Instead she had to sit in a chair and watch TV all the time.

Luckily, she recently found Playaway on the Internet. It is awesome and unique. It's unlike CDs, audio cassettes or downloads. The only thing she needs to do is press play, and then she can to listen to an entire book or a music compilation.

Now she can listen while she is walking, typing, or doing crafts, especially on a rainy day like this day.

In her living room is a big oblong window, and on this rainy day she sits in a chair and watches people walking and cars driving while she listens to *A Little Princess* on Playaway.

A Little Princess by Frances Hodgson Burnett is one of Emily's favourite books. The book about the little girl and her father makes her think of her dad. Her dad treated her like a real princess.

It's quite enjoyable listening to the Playaway alone. Sometimes when she looks out her window she sees car accidents and queer emergency situations. Police often come immediately to solve the problems. She even thinks that it is like a picnic, watching all these things and eating snacks while she listens to the Playaway.

Playaway is really good company, especially for someone like Emily, a lonely, sad girl.

"I won't be alone now, Daddy," she whispers.

THE DOOR

On this burning day, Emily runs into the campus library to cool off.

She sits in her usual seat. She has a cup of tea and then opens her journal.

She starts to write:

> My world changed forever when I lost my innocence. My dear dad always knew what to say, how to handle the situation, and how to comfort me whenever I was upset, angry. I miss him greatly, and I know that I am going through a bit of a hard time since he passed away.
>
> Although I haven't seen my daddy for four years now, I keep thinking about him. I

don't even want to believe that he is gone, and I haven't gotten much sleep at night since his funeral.

I remember my whole family was at his funeral, along with so many of his friends and co-workers. Many of his friends spoke, talking about him and his life. Remembering the eulogies kills my heart. My dad was a superman. Each time I did naughty things, he didn't blame me at all and kept quiet.

Lots of people said to me, "Be strong" and "He wouldn't want you to be sad."

Well, I still struggle with the loss of my father. It's hard to accept the fact that I will never see him again, or hear his voice. Many things remind me of him, and I can't help but smile at the fun things we did. I know he is looking down on me all the time now. He wouldn't want me to cry anymore. He would like me to be happy, so I have tried to have a relationship again with my mother and my brother, but some things are missing—love and trust. It's not 100 percent anymore. We always fight and misunderstand each other. Now, I am thinking that they're just using me, tripping on me. I don't know what to do. My heart and all my life are so sad.

I know that most people are very confused about how my brother could abuse me, the sick and disgusting act that he did to me. They cannot understand completely, because they were never in that situation.

That's the story of my life up to now: sad, useless, worthless, and alone.

I started write about my painful past because I think of myself first now and not my family. Although it makes me cry, hurts me, makes me feel lost and confused when I write down this sadness, I know that finding meaning in suffering is the road to healing.

I am studying at a very charming campus now. I started out well going to all of my classes. I think I am studying a course that could support my goal. I want to study to become a writer. I also feel happier as a student. I just like to tell stories. I hope the stories I tell here don't sound crazy, and I would appreciate it greatly if the readers understand pain and understand why I feel so sad at times. I would also appreciate it if readers pray for me sometimes. Someday the achievements will come to me.

That last paragraph just fit on the last page of Emily's journal. She heaves a long sigh. She closes her journal, packs up, and goes home excited. She is excited for tomorrow's class excursion to the art gallery.

The new journal is waiting for Emily to start from tomorrow the art gallery. It seems that her journal is opening its heart and life is opening its door. I hope she gets her free, clear blue skies under its love.

THE END—EMILY'S DREAM ABOUT LIFE

Emily's Journey 1 is just a memory of her past sadness.

Emily has a dream about her life, since she has gone through such things, and her dream is to learn to be a writer.

Once she has finished a writing course, she will live in a small town where her mum and her brother cannot find her. She will write a story about that town. It may be a romantic town, or an adventurous town, or just an ordinary town. Anyway, she'll get the story written, and then she will find a publisher to publish her book. It might take her a year to finish that book. Then she will move to another town where she would like to write another book, and then she will move to the next town that she would like to write about. She will keep on and on. She hopes it doesn't sound crazy—travelling around and writing and getting little income from it. Actually, she had that kind of life for a month eight years ago, and she was alone. She couldn't continue it because that kind of life was hard for her, since she didn't have much income at that young age. Now, she thinks it would be enough for her to have that kind of life. She had a good father, so she has enough so that she can travel and write. One day when it is time for her to see her dad, she will leave everything to charity.

She knows that this is not reality, but for her, due to her difficult family situation, she wants to escape reality. Fortunately, she had a good father who can make this possible.

Thank you for reading the first journey of Emily. If there is any chance, she would like to present to you the next journey, which contains a fully happy, cheerful life.

~ The End ~

Printed in the United States
By Bookmasters